MW00463948

For my Kelliher aunts: Momo, Trishie, Bambi, Ellen, and Nancy.
Thank you for all the Christmases—JTK

For my parents who put a TV in my bedroom when I was six.
Go Bayside!—AF

PENGUIN WORKSHOP
An imprint of Penguin Random House LLC, New York

First published in the United States of America by Penguin Workshop,
an imprint of Penguin Random House LLC, New York, 2024

Visit us online at penguinrandomhouse.com.

Library of Congress Cataloging-in-Publication Data is available.

Manufactured in China

ISBN 9780593753200   10 9 8 7 6 5 4 3 2 1 HH

A VERY MERRY 90s CHRISTMAS

BY J. T. KELLIHER

ILLUSTRATED BY ALEX FINE

'Twas the night before Christmas
when all through the house
the only sound you could hear
was the click of a mouse.

In the glow of his iMac, his face went dour.
"My absurdly large family should be home by this hour!
A short trip to Disney. Their return flight delayed.
I stayed back for a gig at the Smash Club (we slayed).
But the house feels too quiet. A true controversy.
Me alone on Christmas? Have mercy!"

He typed in his password to America Online.
The internet modem went
DEEE DURRR oooOOOeeeee RHINEEEEEEEE.
Then, lo, on his Buddy List he saw her—
a neighborhood friend named Mrs. Doubtfire.
"Help is on the way, dear!" she typed with glee.
"I'll even invite my dear friend A.C."

A.C. was at home playing *Super Mario 3*.
"I'm so down. Let's make it a big party!
On, Zack! On, Lisa! On, Kelly Kapowski!
On, Screech, on, Jessie, and Principal Belding!
The Bayside Tigers are heading upstate.
Oh, and we should probably bring some dates."

The Spice Girls, he knew, were knackered in Chino.
They were playing keno with Janet Reno.

"Once we're done, we'd love to come!
Can Janet be our plus one?"

Janet called Michael Jordan, who was feeding his Tamagotchi:
"They've got a backyard. We could even play bocce!"

"That's the coolest thing I've ever heard!
I'll even invite a friend from the suburbs!"

"I'm glad you called," Macaulay replied.
"I can't even eat my mac and cheese with these guys.
Can I call a friend I met through the Pigeon Lady?
Her haircut is great, though her lattes are shady."

"This is perfect! I need a trip to take.
My boyfriend just claimed we were on a break?!
Do you mind if I give my friend Whitney a holler?
I'll serve this last cup of coffee and call her."

"You're a dear friend, and I will always love you!
Thanks for the invite. Can Connie Chung come, too?"

"My husband Maury and I are in!
But could we make it a trio?
I'd love to include my dear friend Leo."

"For you, Connie, I can't say no!
Can I bring Kate, too? I'll never let go.
We've just finished filming and are leaving the set.
We can hop aboard a friend's private jet."

"Ironic you called," Alanis said with a snort.
"I actually just ran into someone at the airport.
His name is Dave, if you oughta know.
He and his fam are stranded in Orlando.
Why don't we take my plane to San Francisco?
We can drink Hi-C and listen to Sisqó."

The next morning on Christmas, he was blue.
His cassette player echoed
"All I Want for Christmas Is You."

Then at the door he heard such a noise—
a rush of people, their arms full of toys.
Pogs and Game Boys and Ring Pops a-luster.
Dunkaroos and Yoo-hoos and gift cards to Blockbuster.

There were Furbies and Kirbys and Tickle Me Elmos.
Lisa Frank Trapper Keepers tied up with bows.
And, hark! What was that in Rachel's bag?
A Princess Diana Beanie Baby, still with its tag.

But then he saw them. His greatest gift.
His family walked in and he felt his heart lift.

"All I wanted was you," he said through tears.
"My whole family together. My best friends so dear.
Our house is so full. My joy will never fade."

It was, in the end, the Christmas of the decade.